2

Charg
book i
anothe
you hav

Educational Consultant: Geraldine Taylor

LADYBIRD BOOKS

UK | USA | Canada | Ireland | Australia
India | New Zealand | South Africa

Ladybird Books is part of the Penguin Random House group of companies
whose addresses can be found at global.penguinrandomhouse.com.

ladybird.com

Penguin
Random House
UK

First published 2014. This edition 2016.
001

Printed in China

A CIP catalogue record for this book is available from the British Library

ISBN: 978-0-241-21597-5

Ladybird

I'm Ready... for School!

Written by Amanda Li

Illustrated by Sonia Esplugas

Contents

My Brilliant Body

Your body is made up of lots of parts
that work together.

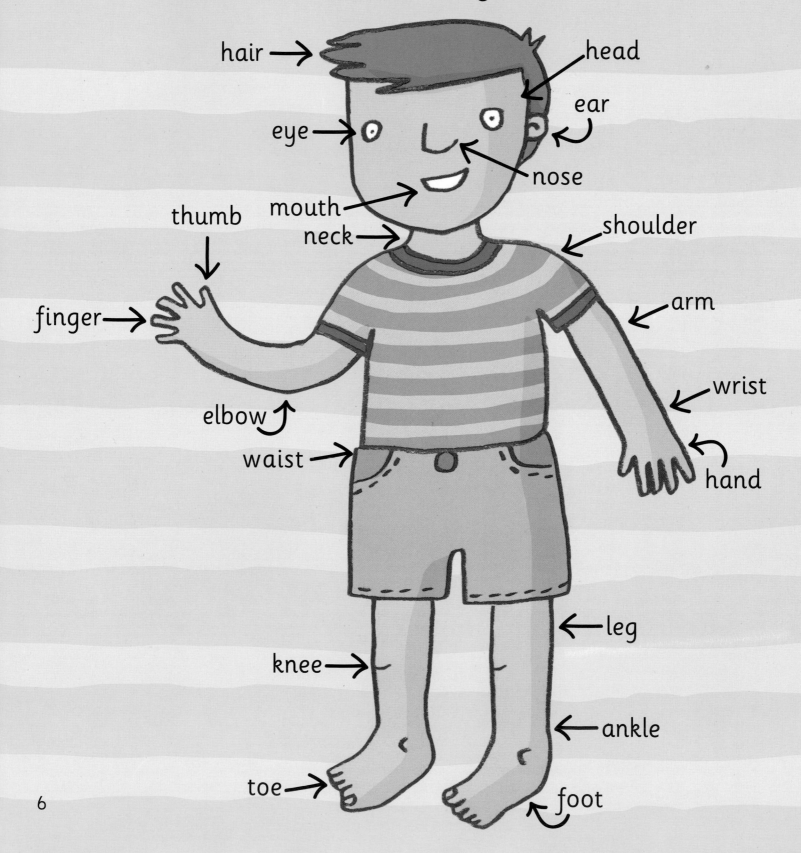

hair →
head
ear
eye →
nose
mouth
thumb
neck →
shoulder
finger →
arm
wrist
elbow
hand
waist →
leg
knee →
ankle
toe →
foot

Here are some of the things the body can do.

skip

hop

run

catch

stomp

dance

throw

jump

clap

What do you like to do?

Let's Get Dressed

Lots of clothes are drying on the washing lines.

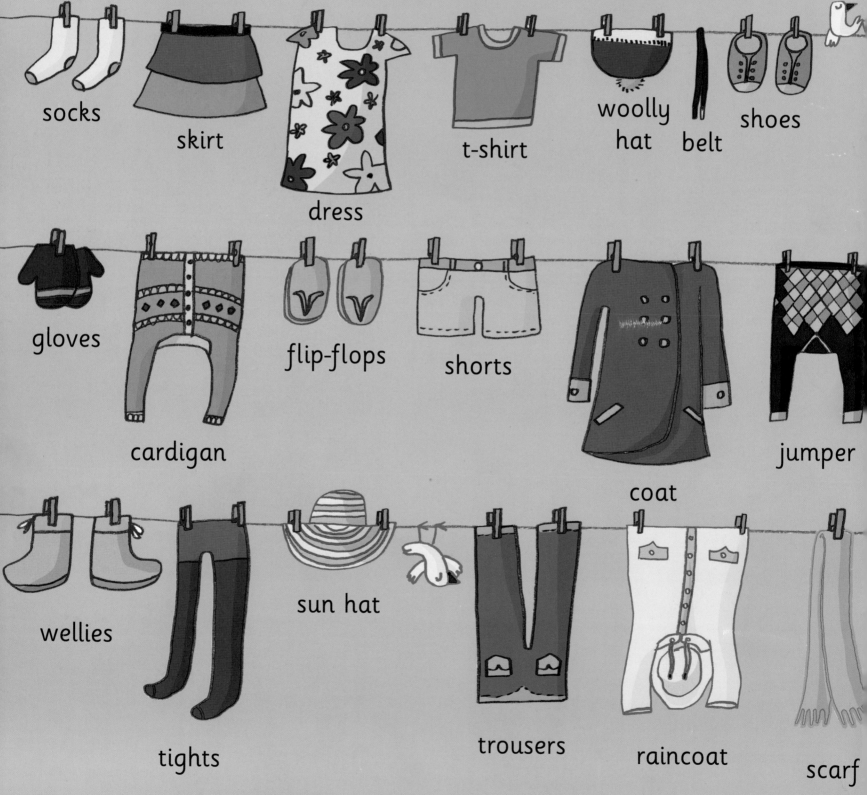

socks

skirt

dress

t-shirt

woolly hat

belt

shoes

gloves

cardigan

flip-flops

shorts

coat

jumper

wellies

tights

sun hat

trousers

raincoat

scarf

Can you
put on
your coat?

Can you
do up
a button?

Can you
put on
your shoes?

Can you
do up
a zip?

Point to the clothes you would wear on:

a hot day   a rainy day   a cold day

My Marvellous Manners

Being polite and having good manners is important.

"You can use my pencil."

I can share

"Please may I have the hoop?"

I can say please

"Thank you for my present."

I can say thank you

"I like to tidy my things away."

I can tidy up

"I'm listening."

I can listen

"It's Isabel's turn first."

I can take turns

"Sorry I knocked you over."

I can say sorry

"Excuse me, may I have a go?"

I can say excuse me

Always remember to say please and thank you.

People Who Help Us

Point to the pictures. Do you know what jobs these people do?

chef

librarian

nurse

shopkeeper

builder

astronaut

doctor

firefighter

police officer

vet

teacher

farmer

What do you want to be when you grow up?

My Favourite Food

Point to the pictures and name
the different foods.

banana

orange

grapes

yoghurt

milk

bread

peas

carrot

sweetcorn

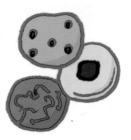

biscuits

pizza

cheese

What is your favourite food?

 apple

 chips

 water

 egg

 cucumber

 tomato

 potato

 strawberry

 fish fingers

 ham

 orange juice

sandwich

Things That Go

Point to the pictures and name the different vehicles you can see.

helicopter

bicycle

motorbike

bus

car

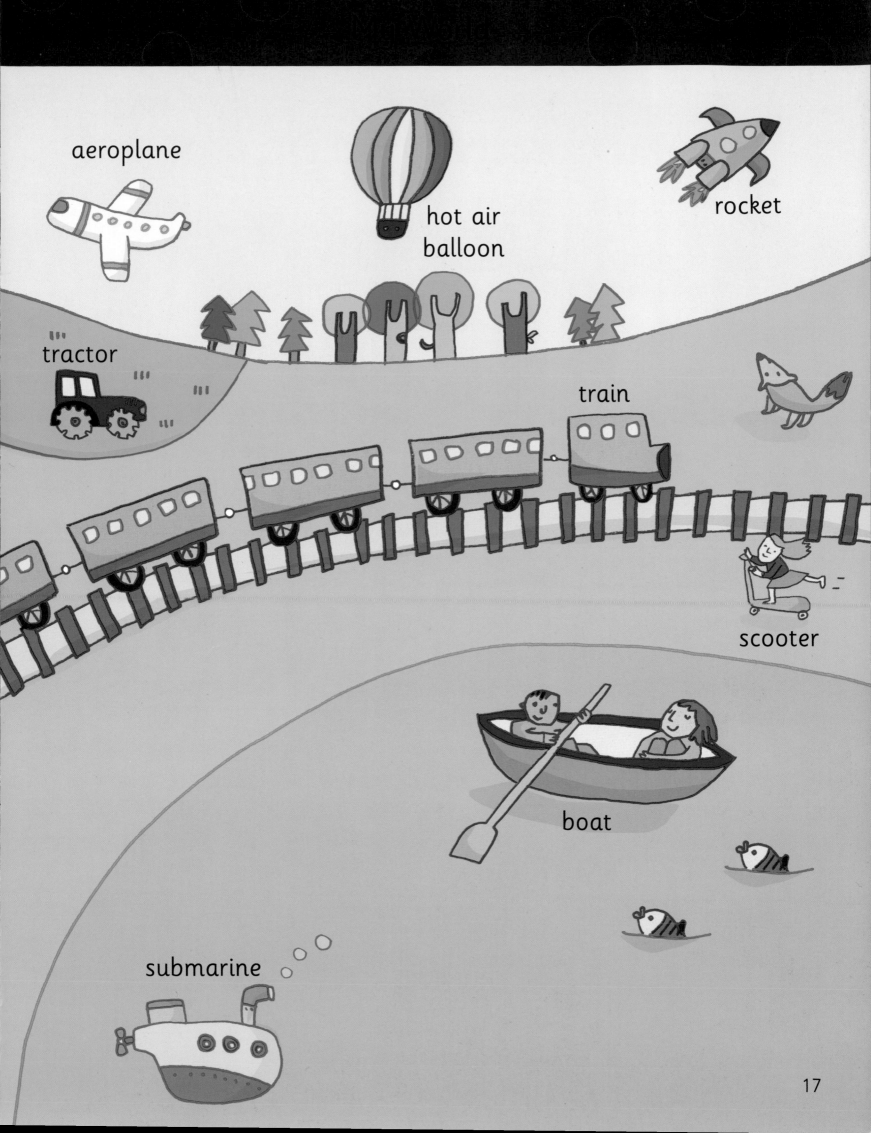

aeroplane

hot air
balloon

rocket

tractor

train

scooter

boat

submarine

Amazing Animals

Point to the pictures and name the different animals you can see.

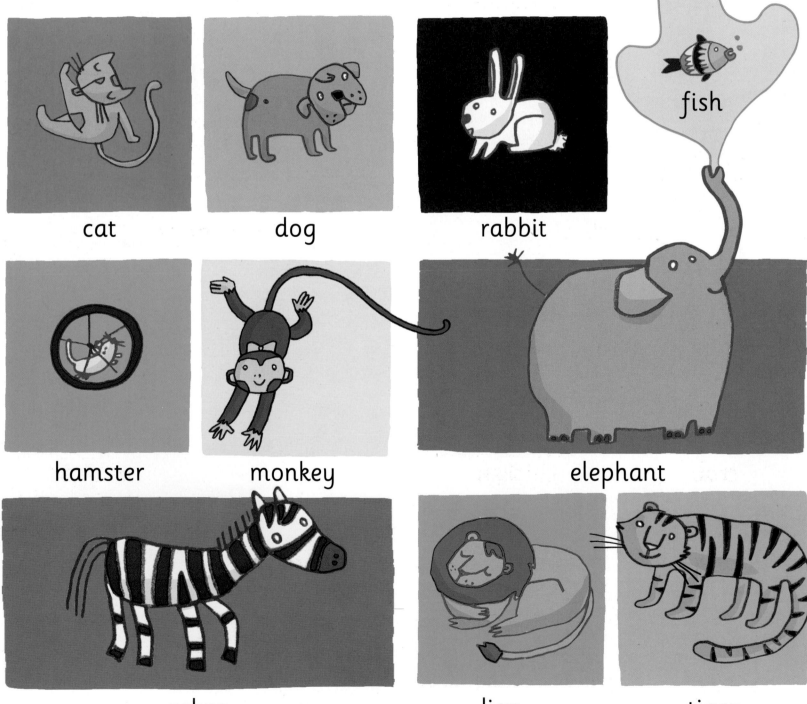

cat

dog

rabbit

fish

hamster

monkey

elephant

zebra

lion

tiger

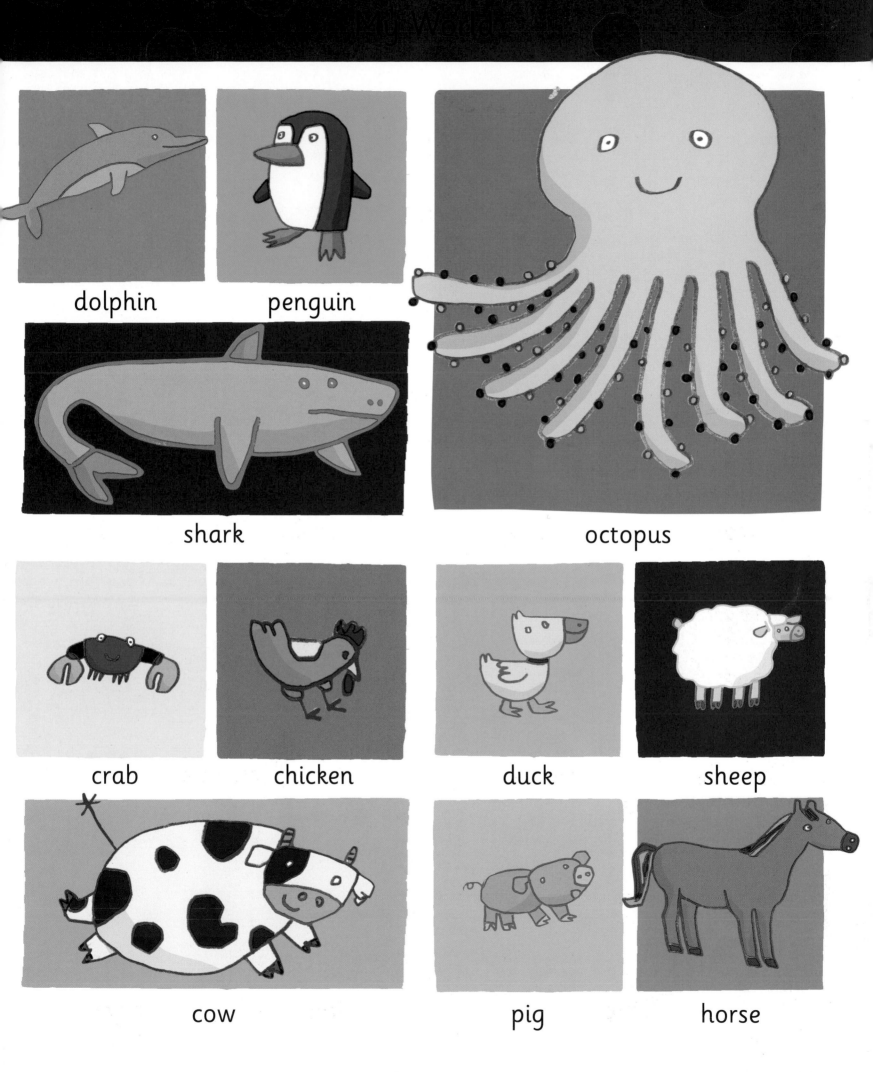

dolphin

penguin

shark

octopus

crab

chicken

duck

sheep

cow

pig

horse

Places I Go

There are lots of places to visit when you are out and about.

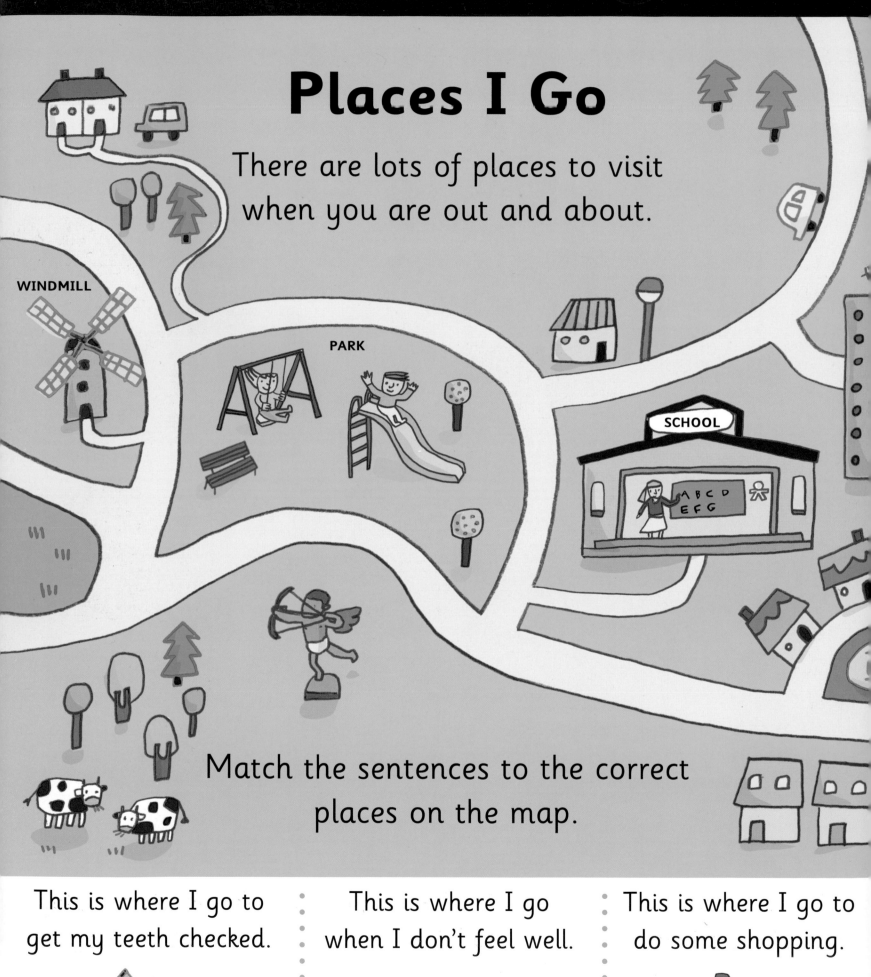

WINDMILL

PARK

SCHOOL

Match the sentences to the correct places on the map.

This is where I go to get my teeth checked.

This is where I go when I don't feel well.

This is where I go to do some shopping.

This is where I go to borrow a book.

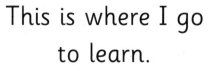

This is where I go to learn.

This is where I play on the slide.

Days of the Week

There are seven days in the week.

Monday	Tuesday	Wednesday	Thursday

Friday	Saturday	Sunday

Point to the pictures and talk about what the children are doing.

Jo is having
a bath.

Ben is getting
dressed.

Kate is eating
her breakfast.

Julia is brushing
her teeth.

John is sleeping
in bed.

Jen is having a
sandwich for lunch.

Jack is
waking up.

Tess is reading
a story.

Ollie is walking
to school.

Months of the Year

There are twelve months in the year.
When is your birthday?

January	**February**	**March**	**April**
May	**June**	**July**	**August**
September	**October**	**November**	**December**

I can remember how many days are in September!

Thirty days has September,
April, June and November;
All the rest have thirty-one,
Except for February alone.
And that has twenty-eight days clear,
And twenty-nine in each leap year.

The Seasons

There are four seasons in the year.
Match the season to the correct picture.

Spring   **Summer**   **Autumn**   **Winter**

Shapes

There are shapes all around you – at home,
at the park and at school.

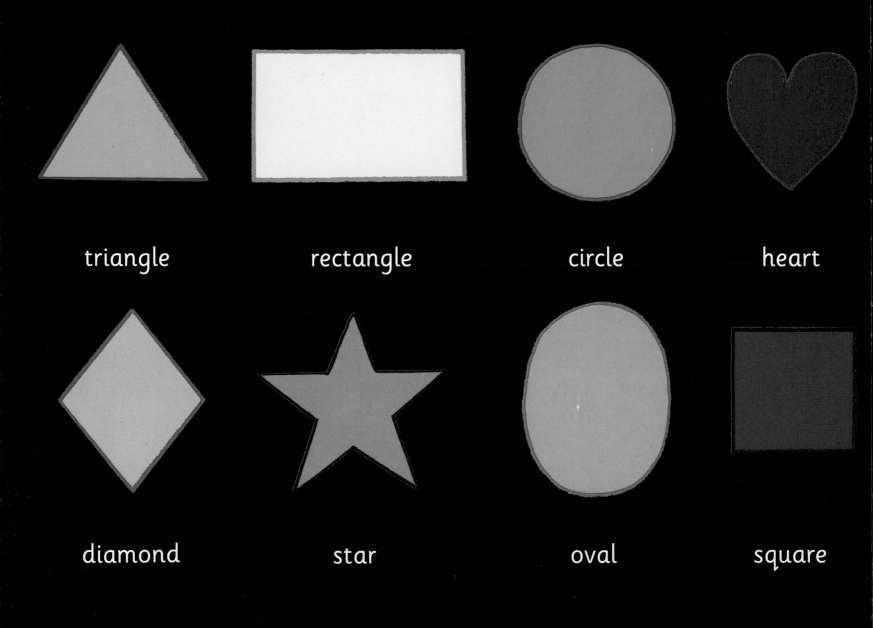

triangle   rectangle   circle   heart

diamond   star   oval   square

Can you name the shapes on the page?

How many different shapes can you find in the picture?

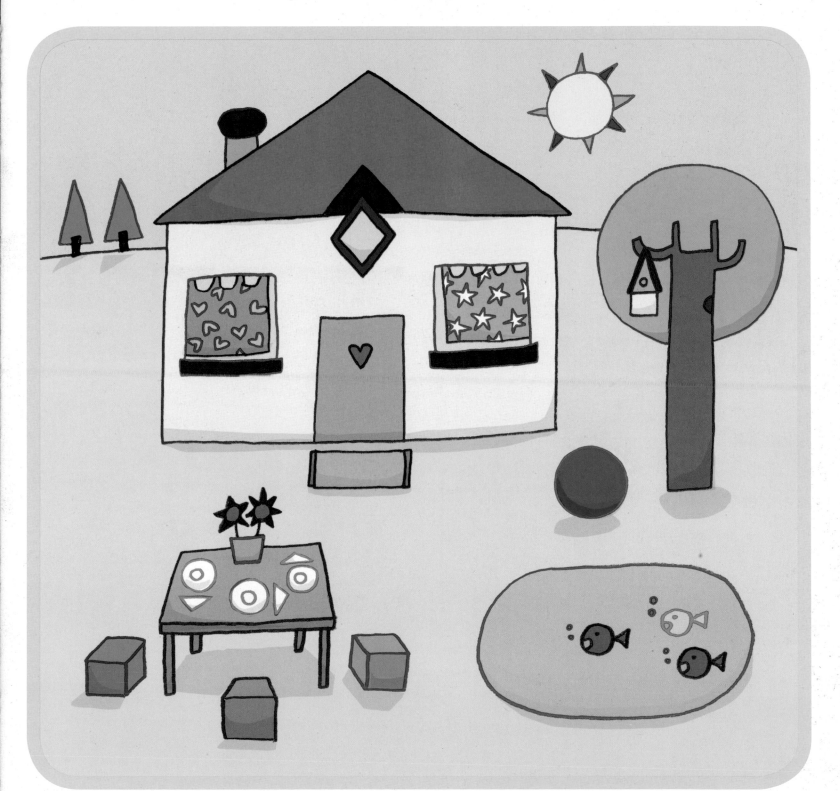

Colours

Point to the different colours in the paintbox.

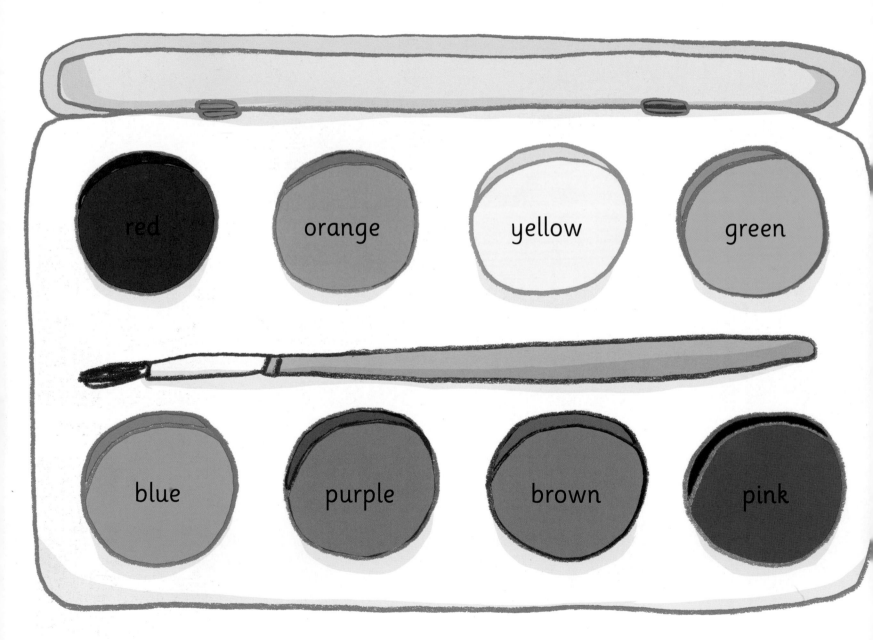

What is your favourite colour?

Look at the pictures. What colour is each toy?

dinosaur

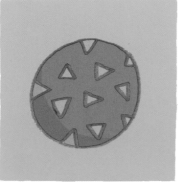

ball

Jack-in-the-box

doll

teddy

tractor

clown

hand puppet

train

wooden blocks

kite

scooter

Opposites

Point to the pictures. Name all the different opposites you can see.

up   down

tall   short

hot   cold

wet   dry

full   empty

open   closed

big

little

new

old

slow

fast

asleep

awake

happy

sad

Count and Play

Let's count from one to ten!
Trace the numbers with your finger.

one	**1**	⚽
two	**2**	🚲 🚲
three	**3**	🛴 🛴 🛴
four	**4**	🛹 🛹 🛹 🛹
five	**5**	🪁 🪁 🪁 🪁 🪁
six	**6**	🎾 🎾 🎾 🎾 🎾 🎾
seven	**7**	🪣 🪣 🪣 🪣 🪣 🪣 🪣
eight	**8**	🔨 🔨 🔨 🔨 🔨 🔨 🔨 🔨
nine	**9**	⚪ ⚪ ⚪ ⚪ ⚪ ⚪ ⚪ ⚪ ⚪
ten	**10**	🍦 🍦 🍦 🍦 🍦 🍦 🍦 🍦 🍦 🍦

This little boy has lost ten ice creams.
Can you help him find them all?

Garden Counting

Let's count from eleven to twenty!
Trace the numbers with your finger.

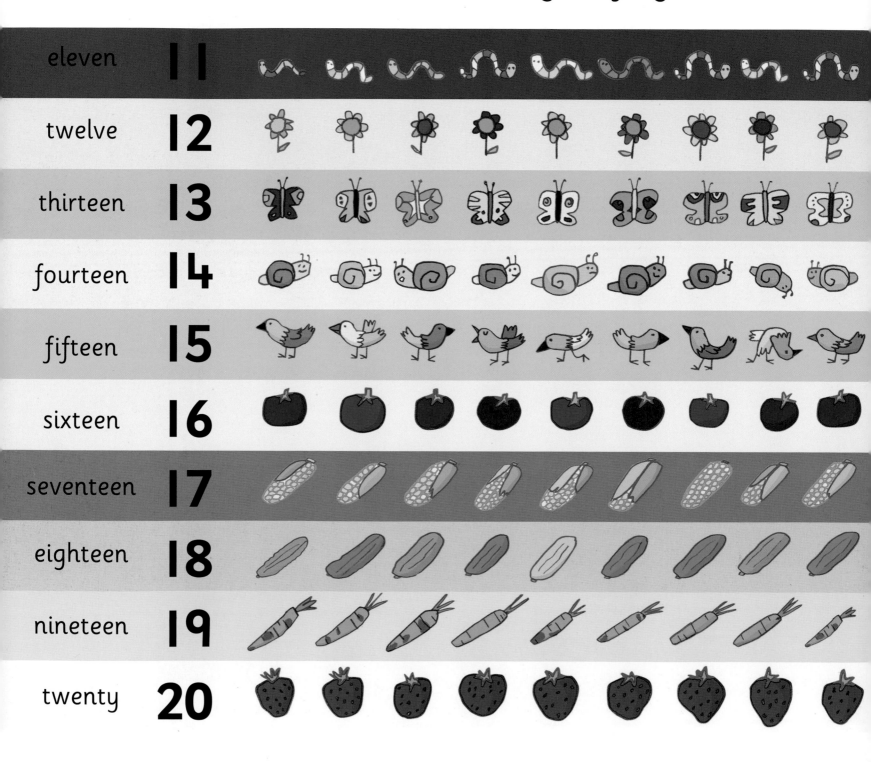

eleven	11
twelve	12
thirteen	13
fourteen	14
fifteen	15
sixteen	16
seventeen	17
eighteen	18
nineteen	19
twenty	20

All About School

The children in your class are
starting school, just like you!

At school there will be:

| friendly teachers | a coat peg | a desk to sit at | new friends |

There will be lots of things to learn:

| I will practise my reading | I will write stories | I will play on the computer | I will learn to swim |

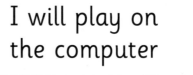

The Alphabet Path

At school you will learn your alphabet and begin to read and write.

Follow the alphabet path with your finger.

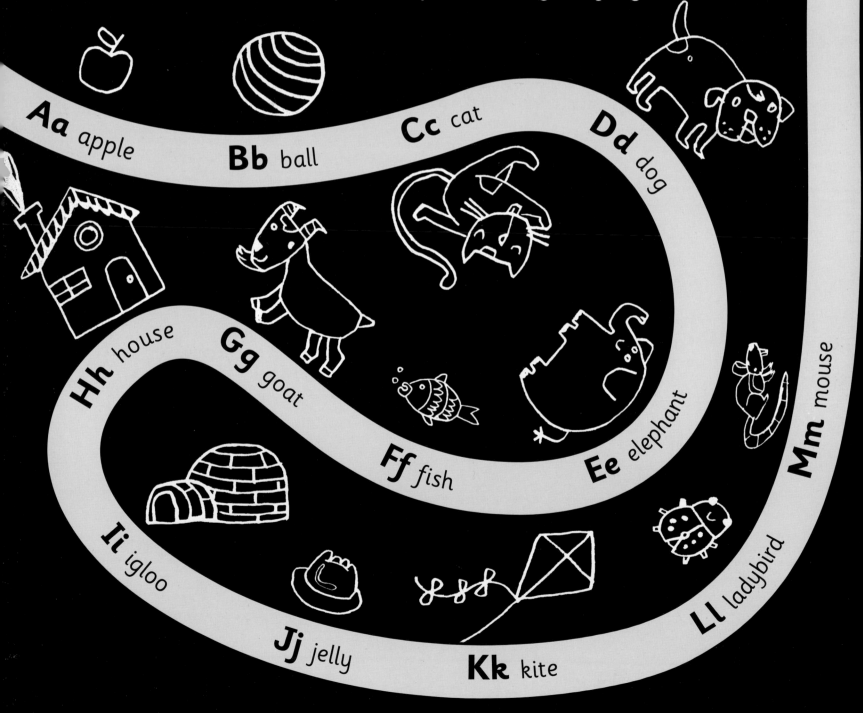

Aa apple

Bb ball

Cc cat

Dd dog

Ee elephant

Ff fish

Gg goat

Hh house

Ii igloo

Jj jelly

Kk kite

Ll ladybird

Mm mouse

Nn net

Oo octopus

Pp penguin

Qq queen

Rr rabbit

Ss snake

Tt teddy

Uu umbrella

Vv van

Ww watch

Xx x-ray

Yy yo-yo

Zz zebra

Do you know which letter your name begins with?
Can you write your name?

It's About Time

We use clocks to help us tell the time. The big hand points to the minutes and the little hand points to the hour.

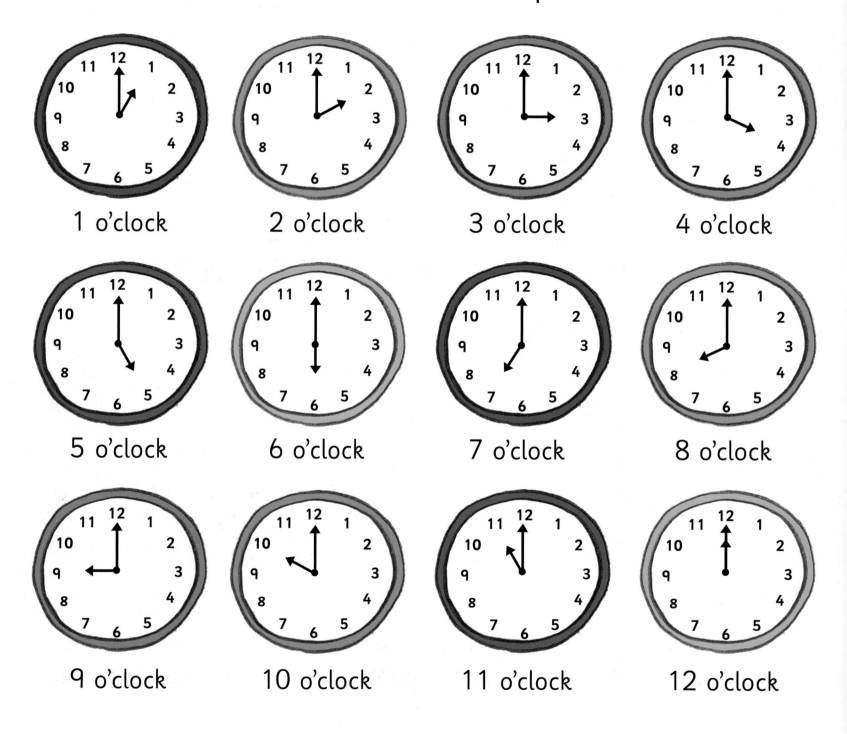

1 o'clock 2 o'clock 3 o'clock 4 o'clock

5 o'clock 6 o'clock 7 o'clock 8 o'clock

9 o'clock 10 o'clock 11 o'clock 12 o'clock

Can you point to 6 o'clock?

Look at the pictures. What are the children doing?

At 8 o'clock
I walk to school.

At 11 o'clock
we play in the playground.

At 1 o'clock
we eat our lunch.

At 2 o'clock
it's storytime.

At 3 o'clock it's
time to go home.

Languages of the World

Have a go at saying 'hello' in these different languages!

German

French

Spanish

English

Italian

Mandarin Chinese

Hindi

Polish

New Experiences

Starting school will feel very new!
There is lots to look forward to:

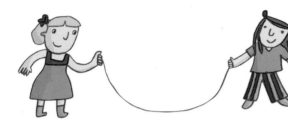

making new friends

learning to read

playing instruments

friendly teachers

drawing and colouring

playing sport

craft activities

lunchtime

storytime

playtime

learning to write

home time

What are you looking forward to about starting school?

Now I'm Ready for School

I get up.

I eat my breakfast.

I brush my teeth.

I get dressed.